better together*

*This book is best read together, grownup and kid.

akidsco.com

a kids book about

a kids book about

by Salvador Bentolila

a kids book about

Text and design copyright © 2023
by A Kids Book About, Inc.

Copyright is good! It ensures that work like this can exist, and more work in the future can be created.

All rights reserved. No part of this publication may be reproduced, distributed, or transmitted in any form or by any means, including photocopying, recording, other electronic or mechanical methods, without the prior written permission of the publisher, except in the case of brief quotations embodied in critical reviews and certain other noncommercial uses permitted by copyright law. For permission requests, write to the publisher.

A Kids Book About, Kids Are Ready, and the colophon 'a' are trademarks of A Kids Book About, Inc.

Printed in the United States of America.

A Kids Book About books are available online: *akidsco.com*

To share your stories, ask questions, or inquire about bulk purchases (schools, libraries, and nonprofits), please use the following email address: *hello@akidsco.com*

ISBN: 978-1-958825-30-3
Ebook ISBN: 978-1-958825-31-0

Designed by Rick DeLucco
Edited by Emma Wolf

To my daughter, for inspiring me
to share this message.

Intro

This book was written to teach kids early on how valuable and important water is in our lives. We interact with water so frequently every day, but do we know enough about it? Where does it come from? What are its different forms? What is it used for? Why is it important?

Explore the answers to these questions within the pages of this book, and you'll even learn some fun facts about water along the way! Did you know that only about 2.5% of all water on our planet is freshwater, and of that about 70% is frozen in glaciers and ice caps? And what happens to the small amount that is left to use?

I hope you and your kids can start important conversations about water in your home. I invite you to practice gratitude for the water we get to use, which keeps us and our planet healthy, but more importantly, I encourage you to take action and conserve it.

How many times have
you used water today?

 **HAVE YOU BRUSHED YOUR TEETH?**

 **HAVE YOU FLUSHED THE TOILET?**

 **HAVE YOU TAKEN A SHOWER?**

 **HAVE YOU HAD A GLASS OF WATER TO DRINK?**

Water is a big part
of our lives every day.

So, what is it?

Water is a necessity for life. It is defined as 1 oxygen and 2 hydrogen atoms, but it's so much more than that.

When water is clean, it doesn't have a smell, taste, or color.

You can find water in

RIVERS, LAKES, OCEANS, AND EVEN OUR BODIES.

Different temperatures can change the form water takes:

when it gets really hot, water turns into a gas, or steam...

and when it's really cold, water can freeze into ice.

WATER IS FOR LOTS OF

IMPORTANT REASONS.

Our bodies are around 60% water, so when we don't drink enough, it makes a big difference!

We might feel really tired, get headaches, feel dizzy, or have darkly-colored urine, which are signs that our body isn't working properly.

BUT DRINKING THE RIG

keeps our skin, eyes, and nose moist. ------

delivers oxygen throughout our body. ------

clears out waste through urine and sweat. ------

WATER DOES SO

HT AMOUNT OF WATER...

maintains our body's temperature, so it can work properly.

protects important parts of our bodies, like the brain and spinal cord.

lubricates our joints, so we can move easily.

MUCH FOR US!

Water is also really important

FOR THE.

PLANET

Water is necessary for...

 crops, so they can grow and feed people all over the world.

 cleaning clothes, dishes, and buildings, so people can stay safe and healthy.

 firefighters, so they can put out fires.

 trees, so they can produce the oxygen we need to breathe.

 animals, so they can live, reproduce, and keep the food chain balanced.

 ships, so they can cross oceans and rivers to move people and products.

Water also lets us have fun swimming, kayaking, snorkeling, or playing waterpolo (like I did as a kid!).

BASICALLY, WATER MATTERS FOR EVERYTHING.

Did you know that our planet is about 70% water?

It's mostly salt water (like the ocean) and some fresh water, which includes water in glaciers, ice caps, groundwater, and surface water.

The groundwater and surface water which we can access make up a really small amount—only about 0.8% of all the water on Earth!*

*That means 99.02% of water isn't available for us to drink or brush our teeth with!

And this tiny amount of water isn't evenly distributed across the planet.

Some areas of the world have way more water than others.

And even if there is water available, some places don't have access to clean water.

Years ago, I traveled to Misuuni, a village in Kenya, Africa, with a volunteer organization to help people get access to clean water.

I saw a lot of people drinking out
of lakes where the water wasn't safe.

This caused people
to get sick and even die.

So our team worked to build a system of pipes and tanks to collect rainwater to use for drinking and washing.

This helped the people in this village live longer and healthier lives, and it saved them so much time.

Before this system, kids spent most of the day going back and forth from the lake to collect water for their families, so they weren't able to go to school.

CAN YOU IMAGINE THAT?

For most of us, we probably turn on the faucets in our homes and don't even think about the water that comes out.

But for many people all over the world, it's a huge sacrifice and time investment just to get a basic, necessary part of living.

The clean water we have is limited and needs to be protected and preserved.

Lots of things can contaminate the water we have and make it unsafe to drink or use like:

- TOXIC CHEMICALS
- FERTILIZERS FROM AGRICULTURE
- OIL SPILLS
- TRASH
- WASTEWATER
  (WATER FROM TOILETS, SHOWERS, AND SINKS)

This is called

and unfortunately, it happens often and everywhere.

For example, some cities have underground pipes that collect both wastewater and rainwater to be treated, or made cleaner.

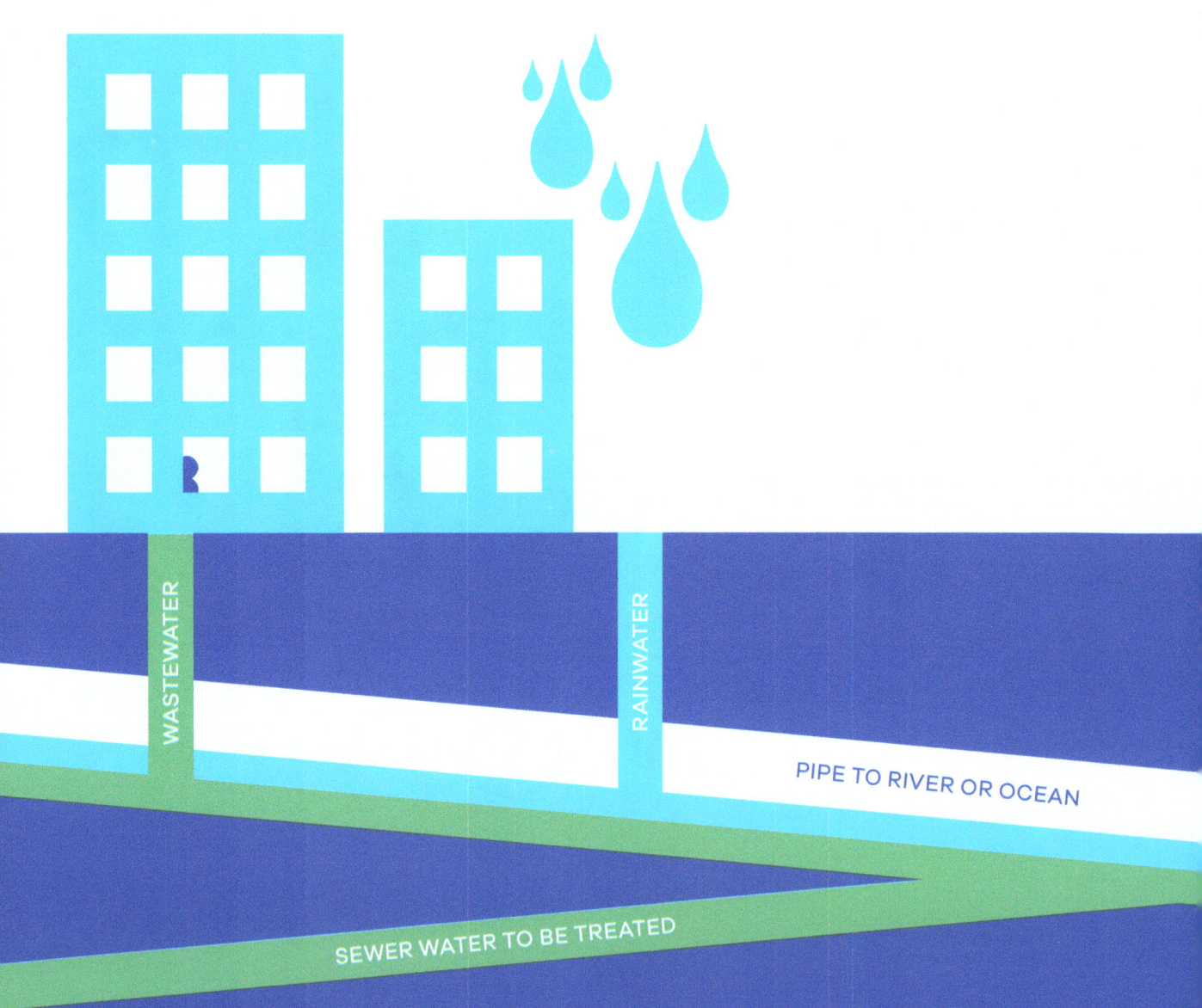

But when it rains a lot, sometimes the untreated wastewater can flow right into a river or nearby body of water, which pollutes it.

Reducing this kind of damage was a big part of the work I did as an engineer in New York.

The impact of minimizing water pollution is huge—it provides cleaner water for humans and animals.

Water is vitally important for all of us.
So, how are we taking care of it
around the world?

There are organizations everywhere working to provide clean water where there isn't any.

Some cities are rebuilding their water systems to improve water quality and divert rainwater to ponds, gardens, and natural parks.

Many companies are creating machines that are more water-efficient—like dishwashers, toilets, and sinks.

SO, WHAT CAN YOU DO TO BE MINDFUL OF HOW YOU USE WATER AND CONSERVE IT FOR OUR FUTURE?

Take shorter showers.

Turn off the tap while brushing your teeth.

Avoid single-use products like plastic straws, forks, and spoons.

Recycle everything you can.

Water supports all life on Earth.

And it's our job to protect it, preserve it, and conserve it so future generations can enjoy it too.

Remember, every drop counts.

Start taking action today!

Outro

Water plays a huge role in our lives and it's our responsibility to take care of it! The good news is you can start taking action today. Here are a few ways to do it.

Try to find ways to conserve water on a daily basis. Wash fruits and vegetables in a container instead of running the faucet, and use buckets instead of a hose to clean your family's cars. Look for opportunities in your area to volunteer at clean-up sites near a beach, lake, or river.

You can also donate to a nonprofit organization. **Charity:Water** and **Engineers Without Borders** are 2 that are close to me. **Water for People** and **Water.org** are examples of other great nonprofits to check out.

Above all, share this book and message with your friends, family, and community so others can be informed and start taking action too. The world will thank you!

About The Author

Salvador Bentolila's (he/him) career has always been related to water. He understood the importance of water after an eye-opening experience in Kenya, where he witnessed people walking long hours to get water and others getting sick or dying because of the quality of that water.

Since then, he has been an advocate of conserving water. Salvador has designed projects to supply water in Africa, managed projects to build water infrastructure in New York, and now implements technology so others can plan, design, build, and operate water-related projects around the world.

He wrote this book to share the importance of water for ourselves and our surroundings, and how we can help conserve it for future generations.

in linkedin.com/in/salvadorbentolila

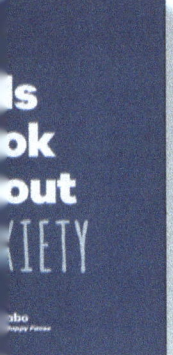    

 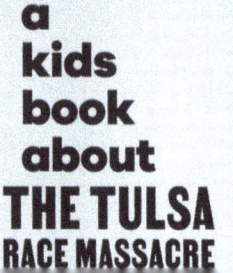

Discover more at **akidsco.com**

www.ingramcontent.com/pod-product-compliance
Lightning Source LLC
Chambersburg PA
CBHW061359010526
44107CB00012B/994